CCEA | GCSE

FRENCH VOCABULARY BOOK 1

Identity, Lifestyle & Culture

COLOURPOINT
EDUCATIONAL

© Diarmuid Brittain and Colourpoint Creative Ltd 2022

ISBN: 978 1 78073 253 4

First Edition
First impression

Layout and design: April Sky Design
Printed by: GPS Colour Graphics Ltd, Belfast

The Author

Diarmuid Brittain taught French for 26 years at Grosvenor Grammar School, Belfast. He is also an A level French Examiner for an awarding body.

He lives with his wife and three children in Belfast and remains a Francophile through and through.

This book has borrowed inspiration from hundreds of pupils over the years and it is dedicated to each and every language student and teacher that has graced the doors of Grosvenor Grammar School.

COLOURPOINT EDUCATIONAL

Colourpoint Educational
An imprint of Colourpoint Creative Ltd
Colourpoint House
Jubilee Business Park
21 Jubilee Road
Newtownards
County Down
Northern Ireland
BT23 4YH

Tel: 028 9182 0505
E-mail: sales@colourpoint.co.uk
Website: www.colourpoint.co.uk

This book has been written to help students preparing for the GCSE French specification from CCEA. While Colourpoint Educational and the author have taken every care in its production, we are not able to guarantee that the book is completely error-free. Additionally, while the book has been written to closely match the CCEA specification, it is the responsibility of each candidate to satisfy themselves that they have fully met the requirements of the CCEA specification prior to sitting an exam set by that body. For this reason, and because specifications change with time, we strongly advise every candidate to avail of a qualified teacher and to check the contents of the most recent specification for themselves prior to the exam. Colourpoint Educational therefore cannot be held responsible for any errors or omissions in this book or any consequences thereof.

Contents

Introduction   4

1: **Moi-même, ma famille, les relations, les choix**   6
[Myself, my family, relationships, choices]

2: **Décrire les personnes**   10
[Describing people]

3: **Les réseaux sociaux**   14
[Social media]

4: **Les nouvelles technologies**   16
[New technologies]

5: **Les loisirs**   19
[Free time and leisure]

6: **Les passetemps**   23
[Hobbies]

7: **Les animaux**   26
[Animals]

8: **Les achats et les vêtements**   29
[Shopping and clothes]

9: **La bijouterie**   33
[The Jewellery shop]   *[Not on the CCEA core vocabulary list]*

10: **La papetrie**   34
[The stationery shop] [Not on the CCEA core vocabulary list]

11: **La routine quotidienne**   35
[Daily routine]

12: **La routine quotidienne – quelques verbes**   37
[Daily routine – some verbs]

13: **Les coutumes, les fêtes et les célébrations**   40
[Customs, festivals and celebrations]

Introduction

This is one of four books that form a resource for English-speaking students of French and which seeks to promote **student-led vocabulary acquisition**. It is designed to **promote independent learning** and **free up teacher time**. While it is tailored for GCSE students, it is a powerful resource for all English-speaking students of French.

What do the books cover?

Various GCSE French syllabi (CCEA, WJEC, Edexcel, AQA, OCR) have common vocabulary lists. While this resource makes specific reference to the CCEA specification, it covers the vocabulary listed in all these syllabi and can be used with all of them.

The resource is divided into four books, the first three of which cover the three areas of core vocabulary as presented in the GCSE syllabi:
1. Identity, Lifestyle and Culture (this book)
2. Local, National, International and Global Areas of Interest
3. School Life, Studies and the World of Work

The resource is completed by a fourth book:
4. Verbs, Conjunctions and Other Useful Phrases, which includes an alphabetical list of the most common verbs in French, as well as a list of common connectors, *la Colle Française* (French glue).

Why these books?

- These books are designed to be used independently by students.
- Traditionally, students have been given lists of vocabulary to learn without pronunciation guides and without *aide-mémoires*. With these books, teachers can hand vocabulary learning over to their students, giving the teacher more time to focus on the challenging grammar that requires teacher-led pedagogy.
- Research shows that pupils prefer to learn from hard copies.
- Pupils can have a sense of ownership of this a resource because they can annotate it.
- The most recent GCSE CCEA specification (first examined in 2017) places more emphasis on Listening and Reading, demanding a higher level of vocabulary acquisition.
- This resource can be used independently by students from Year 8 onwards, building over five years to GCSE success. This is particularly useful for schools that need to use remote learning from time to time.

What is the structure of this book?

The vocabulary in the book is presented in the same order as it is presented in the CCEA GCSE syllabus, i.e. in alphabetical order by the English meaning.

Each word has a **pronunciation guide**. The benefits of this are the following:

- Learners can check their pronunciation of the word.
- Learners can test understanding from looking only at the pronunciation guide, thereby improving their listening skills.
- Learners can test themselves on how to write – in correct French – the phonetically described word, thereby improving the accuracy of their writing.
- Learners can work in pairs to test each other orally from English to French and/or French to English.

Most words also have an ***aide-mémoire***. *Aide-mémoire* is French for 'memory aid'. People often struggle under the burden of learning vocabulary, and take little pleasure from the task.

It is the author's belief that if a student can find links between their own language and a foreign one, it makes the process of vocabulary acquisition more of a journey of discovery than a drudgery, and importantly, it allows the learner to hook the foreign words onto words that have already been assimilated in their brain.

The author likes to work with the premise 'words can make you laugh!' There are a number of attempts to be humorous throughout the book, in an effort to link works to the mind of the student. Learners may describe these attempts as 'dad jokes' – but the author believes that learners secretly like them!

The book also includes sections entitled **Practise!** These allow students to practise what they have learned, embedding their learning. Teachers will also find these sections useful in order to set homework or cover work.

What are the tick boxes for?

Each word has three tick boxes. These are provided in order to give the student a way to track their progress and organise their learning. The author suggests the following approach, though you can use whatever method works for you:

- Tick the first box when you have learned the word for the first time. When you are organising your revision use this tick to indicate to yourself what you have covered.
- When you come back later to check that you have retained the word, you can tick the second box.
- By the time you go in to your GCSE exams, you should have been able to tick the third box, to show that you have embedded that word in your brain.

Abbreviations

The book uses the following abbreviations:

(m)	masculine	e.g. *Un garçon*, a boy
(f)	feminine	e.g. *Une fille*, a girl
(m/f)	masculine or feminine	e.g. *Un/une professeur*, a teacher
(mpl)	masculine plural	e.g. *Des garçons*, (some) boys
(fpl)	feminine plural	e.g. *Des filles*, (some) girls

1. Moi-même, ma famille, les relations, les choix
[Myself, my family, relationships, choices]

Word or phrase	Pronunciation guide	Aide-mémoire	English meaning	Check
Adulte (m)	ah-doolt		Adult	
Tante (f)	tawnt	T**au**nt	Aunt	
Bébé (m)	bay-bay		Baby	
Naissance (f)	ness-aw-seuh	**Na**tivity, **na**tal are birth-related	Birth	
Né(e/s) le quatre février	nay leuh (kaatr fay-vree-ay)	**N**ativity, **n**atal are birth-related	Born on the 4th February	
Frère (m)	frair	Friar (Brother) Tuck, Frère Jacques (Brother John) fraternal, fraternity	Brother	
Garçon (m)	gaar-saw	Gar**ç**on – the second part of the word is like son. Traditionally a garçon is a young waiter.	Boy	
Enfant (m)	aw-faw	An in-fant sounds like it	Child	
Couple (m)	kouh-pleuh		Couple	
Cousine (f)	kouh-zeen		Cousin (female)	
Cousin (m)	kouh-zah		Cousin (male)	
Cousins (mpl)	kouh-zah		Cousins	
Garde (f)	gaar-d	Those who **gu**ard the child have the custody	Custody	
Fille (f)	fee-yeuh	A filly is a young female horse, a daughter horse	Daughter	
Divorcé(e/s)	dee-voar-say	Divorcé looks like the English. An 'é' at the end of a verb is generally, 'ed'.	Divorced	
Aîné(e) (m/f)	en-ay	**Ain**ci**e**nt – eldest	Eldest	
Famille (f)	fah-mee-yeuh		Family	
Père (m)	pair	Paternal, papa, pa	Father	
Prénom (m)	pray-naw	Pre-name is a forename and 'nom' looks like name	Forename	
Ami(e) (m/f)	ah-mee	Amicable, amiable both mean friendly	Friend	
Copine (f)	koh-peen	Companion, friend	Friend (female)	
Copain (m)	koh-pah	Companion, friend	Friend (male)	
Fille (f)	fee-yeuh	A filly is a young female horse, a girl horse	Girl	
Filleule (f)	fee-yeul	Linked to filly, a young female horse	Goddaughter	
Parrain (m)	pah-rah	Parrain looks like père, father, this father reigns (rains)	Godfather	
Marraine (f)	mah-ren	Marraine looks like mother, this mother reigns (-raine)	Godmother	
Filleul (m)	fee-yeul	Filial relationship with a son	Godson	
Petits-enfants (mpl)	peuh-teeze aw-faw	Small children are actually grand-children	Grandchildren	
Grand-père (m)	graw-pair	P**ater**nal is to do with the father	Grandfather	

Word or phrase	Pronunciation guide	Aide-mémoire	English meaning	Check
Grand-mère (f)	graw-mair	**Mèr**e – like mother	Grandmother	
Grands-parents (mpl)	graw-pah-raw		Grandparents	
Demi-frère (m)	deuh-mee frair	**Demi** is like semi, semi-circle, half circle	Half-brother	
Demie-soeur (f)	deuh-mee sir	**Demie** is like semi, semi-circle, half circle	Half-sister	
Mari (m)	mah-ree	A **mar**r**i**ed man is a husband	Husband	
Amour (m)	ah-mouhr	Am – is included in words to do with love, e.g. amiable, amicable, amourous	Love	
Homme (m)	awm	**Homo** sapiens is a man	Man	
Marié(e/s)	mah-ree-ay	**Mar**r**i**ed	Married	
Mère (f)	mair	Mare – mother horse, maternal	Mother	
Nom (m)	naw	Name as in the main name, the family or surname	Name (family name)	
Neveu (m)	neuh-veuh	**Ne**ph**e**w	Nephew	
Nouveau-Né (m)	nouh-voh nay	Nouveau – new, like art-nouveau, new art. Né – linked to **n**atal, birth.	Newborn	
Surnom (m)	sir-naw	Sur – on or above. Surnom – a name that is used above, or before, your original name.	Nickname	
Nièce (f)	nee-yess		Niece	
Conjoint(e/s)	kaw-jwah/ kaw-jwaant	Con is Latin for 'with', like chilli con carne, chilli with meat. Joint – joined, joined with.	Non-married partner	
Union Libre (f)	ooh-nyaw lee-breuh	Union – togetherness. Libre – liberated, free from marital vows, pledges	Non-married relationship	
Concubinage (m)	kaw-koo-bee-nah-zheuh	Concubine is the old word for a non-married partner	Non-married union	
Fils (m)/Fille (f) Unique	feese/fee-yeuh ooh-neek	Unique means there is only one of it	Only son, daughter	
Parents (mpl)	pah-raw		Parents	
Partenaire (m)	par-ten-air		Partner	
Rapports (mpl)	rah-pore	Rapport, a good rapport, a good relationship with.	Relationship	
Séparé(e/s)	say-pah-ray	**Separat**ed	Separated	
Célibataire (s)	say-lee bah-tair	Celibate describes someone who does not engage in sexual activity, single	Single	
Soeur (f)	sir	Sorority	Sister	
Fils (m)	feese (like geese)	A filial relationship is a relationship with a son	Son	
Gendre (m)	zhawn-dreuh	Gender male, ironically gene is mentioned but no genes are shared here	Son-in-law	
Belle-Fille (f)	bell-fee-yeuh	A step called Belle before the daughter (filly is a young female horse)	Step-daughter/ daughter-in-law	
Beau-Fils (m)	boh-feese	A step called Beau before the fils (a filial relationship is with a son)	Step-son/ son-in-law	

Word or phrase	Pronunciation guide	Aide-mémoire	English meaning	Check		
Beau-Père (m)	boh-pair	A step called Beau before the père	Step-father/ father-in-law			
Belle-Mère (f)	bell mair	A step called Belle before the mère	Step-mother/ mother-in-law			
Ensemble (s)	aw-sawm-bleuh	An ensemble, a suit (clothes that go together) or musicians playing together, assembly	Together			
Jumelle (f)	zhoo-mel	Gemini are twins in the zodiac, **j**oined	Twin female			
Jumeau (m)	zhoo-moh	Gemini are twins in the zodiac, **j**oined	Twin male			
Jumeaux (mpl)	zhoo-moh	Gemini are twins in the zodiac, **j**oined	Twins (mpl/m&f)			
Jumelles (fpl)	zhoo-mel	Gemini are twins in the zodiac, **j**oined	Twins (fpl)			
Oncle (m)	awn-kleuh		Uncle			
Femme (f)	fam	A female, feminine	Wife			
Veuve (f)	veuhv	**V**idow, with an 'e' to make it feminine	Widow			
Veuf (m)	veuhf	**V**idower, without an 'e' to make it masculine	Widower			
Femme (f)	fam	A female, feminine	Woman			
Cadet (m) / Cadette (f)	cad-ay / cadet	A cadet is a young version of a senior position, e.g. Army cadet	Youngest			

Practise!

1. Combien de personnes est-ce qu'il y a dans ta famille? (How many people are there in your family?)

   Answer with: *Dans ma famille, il y a* .... (**mon** for singular males or singular females starting with a vowel / **ma** for singular females / **mes** for plural, including males and females both together).

   > **Examples**
   >
   > *Dans ma famille, il y a mon père, ma mère, mes deux frères et moi. Je n'ai pas de sœurs. Il y aussi ma tante avec qui je suis très proche. Elle fait partie de ma famille.*
   >
   > > In my family there is my father, my mother, my two brothers and me. I don't have any sisters. There is also my aunt, with whom I am very close. She is part of my family.
   >
   > *Dans ma famille, il n'y a que moi et ma mère. Je suis enfant unique.*
   >
   > > In my family, there are only me and my mother. I am an only child.

   Ta réponse (Your answer): _____

   _____

   _____

   _____

   _____

2. Now, try to write out a list of family members, either for your own family or a celebrity family, using as many of the terms for family members as possible. An example is given below.

   > **Example**
   > For Prince Archie (member of the British Royal Family):
   >
   > | Prince Harry | Megan Markle | Prince William | Kate Middleton | |
   > |---|---|---|---|---|
   > | *Père* | *Mère* | *Oncle* | *Tante* | |
   > | Princess Anne | Prince Charles | Diana Spencer | Prince Andrew | Prince Edward |
   > | *Grand-tante* | *Grand-père* | *Grand-mère* | *Grand-oncle* | *Grand-oncle* |

2: Décrire les personnes
[Describing people]

Word or phrase	Pronunciation guide	Aide-mémoire	English meaning	Tick
Actif(ive)	ak-teef ak-teev		Active	
Fâché(e/s)	fash-ay	Necrotising **fasc**iitis – is the name for the **angry** flesh-eating infection	Angry	
Casse-pieds	kass-pee-yeah	'Casse-pieds' – 'break-feet'. Annoying (pied, pedestrian), fri**cassé** in cooking, broken up.	Annoying	
Pénible(s)	pay-neeb-leuh	Painful	Annoying	
Embêtant (e/s),	awm-bet-aw, amw-bet-awnt	Bête – beast. Embeasting would mean to 'make as a beast', or to be annoying.	Annoying	
De taille moyenne	deuh tie mwy-enn	De – of medium cut, taille, tailor, a cutter of cloth, **m**oy**e**n, **m**e**d**ium	Average height	
Barbe (f)	barb	Goats got cooked on a barbe-à-queue, a spit going from beard to tail (barbe à queue)	Beard	
Belle fille (f)	bell fee-yeuh	Belle – beautiful, bella is Italian for beautiful	Beautiful girl	
Gros garçon (m)	groh gaar-saw	**Gros**s is associated with big, gross pay is big pay before tax	Big boy	
Grosse fille (f)	gross fee-yeuh	**Gross**e, associated with big, fille, filly, young girl horse	Big girl	
Les cheveux (mpl) noirs	lay sheuh-veuh nwaar	Noirs, an anagram of snoir which is almost snore, which happens in the dark	Black hair	
Les yeux (mpl) bleus	lays yeuh bleuh	Eyes and yeux linked with the 'y' and 'e'. Bleu and blue are clearly linked.	Blue eyes	
Barbant(e/s)	baar-baw, bar-bawnt	Barbe – beard. As interesting as a beard growing – i.e. not interesting.	Boring	
Les yeux (mpl) marron	lays yeuh maar-aw	**Mar**oo**n** is reddy-brown	Brown eyes	
Les yeux (mpl) bruns	lays yeuh brah	Looks like brown	Brown eyes	
Dynamique (s)	dee-na-meek	Dynamic	Busy, driven	
Charactéristiques (f)	caar-ak-tay-reese-teek	Charactérstiques physiques – physical characteristics	Characteristics	
Les cheveux (mpl) châtains	lay sheuh-veuh shah-tah	Châtain – ch of chestnut-brown	Chestnut brown hair	
Maladroit(e/s)	mahl-ah-drwaat	Mal – bad (malpractice). 'À droite' is 'on the right'. Bad on the right, up the left, clumsy.	Clumsy	
Confiant(e/s)	kaw-fee-aw, kaw-fee-awnt	Add a 'd' in the middle	Confident	
Les cheveux (mpl) frisés	lay sheuh-veuh free-zay	**Friz**zy hair is tight, curly hair	Curly	
Mort/s, morte/s	morh, mohrt	**Mor**bid, **mor**gue, post-**mort**em	Dead	
Énergique(s)	ay-nair-zheek	**Energe**tic, watch for the lack of 't' in French	Energetic	
Fidèle(s)	fee-dell	Fidelity is faithfulness, infidelity is unfaithfulness	Faithful	

Word or phrase	Pronunciation guide	Aide-mémoire	English meaning	Tick
Plein(e/s) de vie	plah, plen deuh vee	Re**plein**ished is full, of, life. Life is linked to **vi**tal, **vi**vid, **vi**brant.	Full of life	
Marrant(e/s)	mah-raw, mah-rawnt	Mirth is laughter, laughing on Mars	Fun (adjective)	
Généreux, généreuse(s)	zhay-nay-reuh, zhay-nay-reuhz	**Gener**ous	Generous	
Les cheveux (mpl) roux	lay sheuh-veuh rou	Roux – russet, rust coloured	Ginger hair	
Lunettes (fpl)	loo-net	Lune – moon, as in lunar. Lunettes are little moons, the shape of glasses.	Glasses	
Amusant(e/s)	ah-moo-zaw, ah-moo-zawnt	Amusing	Good fun	
Les yeux (mpl) verts	lays yeuh vair	Verdant means green and luscious. **Ye**ux – e**ye**s.	Green eyes	
Beau garçon (m)	boh gaar-saw	Beau is half of beau-tiful	Handsome boy	
Heureux, heureuse(s)	euh-reuh, euh-reuhz	**H**appy, heure means 'hour', as in happy hour	Happy	
Travailleur(s) (-euse/s)	trah-vye-euhr, trah-vye-euhz	**Tr**ials, travails, tribulations are all about hard work, trial of endurance	Hard-working	
Serviable(s)	sair-vee-ahb-leuh	Serving others	Helpful	
Coléreux, coléreuse(s)	kall-ay-reuh, kall-ay-reuhz	**Col**ic makes babies hot-tempered	Hot-tempered	
Impatient(s), impatiente(s)	am-pass-yaw, am-pass-yawnt		Impatient	
Intelligent(e/s)	ahn-tell-ee-zhaw, -zhawnt		Intelligent	
Intéressant(e/s)	ahn-tay-ress-awe, -awnt		Interesting	
Gentil/s, gentille/s	zhawn-tee, zhawn-tee-yeuh	**Gent**le people tend to be kind	Kind	
Paresseux (euse/s)	pah-ress-eu, pah-ress-euhz	A lazy holiday in **Paress**	Lazy	
Vif/s, vive/s	veef, veev	**Viv**id and **vi**brant and **viv**acious are all about being full of life, lively	Lively	
Long/s, longue/s	law, lawn-geuh		Long	
Les cheveux (mpl) longs	lay sheuh-veuh lawh		Long hair	
Mi-longs	mee-lawh	**Me**dium **long**	Medium length	
Méchant(e/s)	may-shaw, may-shawnt	**Cha**rming. Mé reverses the meaning, so méchant is uncharming, naughty, nasty.	Naughty, nasty	
Nerveux(euse/s)	nair-veuh, nair-veuze		Nervous	
Nez (m)	nay	**N**asal	Nose	
Vieil(s), vieux, vieille(s)	vee-yay, vee-yeuh, vee-yay-yeuh	**Ve**nerable suggests experience and age	Old	
Extraverti(e/s)	extra-vair-tea	Extrovert	Outgoing	
Personalité (f)	pair-sawn-aal-eat-ay		Personality	
Joli(e/s)	zhoh-lee	Jolly can be used to mean pretty, it is at least smiley and appealing, jolly pretty	Pretty	

Word or phrase	Pronunciation guide	Aide-mémoire	English meaning	Tick	
Tranquille(s)	traw-keel	Tranquil means calm	Quiet, calm		
Fiable(s)	fee-ahb-leuh	Able, rely-able, able to rely	Reliable		
Triste(s)	treest	**Te**ars are linked to sadness	Sad		
Égoïste(s)	ay-go-east	Egotistical	Selfish		
Altruiste(s)	all-true-east	**Al**l **tru**e to oneself. Doing the right thing. Being selfless.	Selfless		
Sens (m) de l'humour	sawze deuh loo-mouhr		Sense of humour		
Sérieux, sérieuse(s)	say-ree-euh, say-ree-euhz		Serious		
Les cheveux (mpl) courts	lay sheuh-veuh core	Cheveux rhymes with eyes (i.e. yeux, pronounced yeuh) but is longer. A bit curt is a bit short with someone.	Short hair		
Timide(s)	tea-mead	Timid	Shy		
Fille mince (f)	fee-yeuh maass	A strand of mince is slim	Slim girl		
Petit garçon (m)	peuh-tee gaar-saw		Small boy		
Petite fille (f)	peuh-teet fee-yeuh	A petite girl is a small girl	Small girl		
Sportif/s, sportive/s	spor-teef, spor-teeve	**Sport**y	Sporty		
Les cheveux raides	lay sheuh-veuh red	Raides – raid – almost rhymes with straight (careful, pronounced, 'red')	Straight hair		
Bête(s)	bet	'Ê' indicates that the next letter should be 's'. **Be**ast – beasts are seen as a little stupid.	Stupid/silly		
Bavard(e/s)	baah-vaar, baah-vaard	Bah bah bleat bleat bah bah	Talkative		
Grand garçon (m)	graw gaar-saw	Grand is not small. Garçon sounds a bit like 'our son'.	Tall boy		
Grande fille (f)	grawnd fee-yeuh	Grande is not small. Fille – a filly is a young female horse.	Tall girl		
Garçon maigre (m)	gaar-saw meh greuh	A meagre living is a poor living, not plentiful, thin	Thin boy		
Laid(e/s)	lay, led	Laid – same number of letters, the 'd' is not very pretty	Ugly		
Injuste(s)	ah-zhoost	Not just, no justice, not fair	Unfair, unjust		
Jeune(s)	zheuhn	Juvenile, junior, re**juven**ate are all to do with youth	Young		
Les cheveux bouclés	lay sheuh-veuh bou-klay	Boucles – buckle, a buckle is wavy, like a wavy curl	Wavy (not tight, curly)		

Practise!

1. Draw these people:

Il a les cheveux noirs et longs et il est gros et il porte des lunettes.	Elle est petite et elle a les cheveux noirs et courts et elle a trois yeux.

2. Translate the following into French.

He has green eyes and medium length wavy hair. He is sporty and he is energetic but he can be lazy sometimes (de temps en temps).

_____

_____

_____

She is impatient and she is very annoying. She has blue eyes and she has short blond hair. She is confident but she is also clumsy from time to time.

_____

_____

_____

They (m) are interesting and fun but they can be (ils peuvent être) hot-tempered and silly but I like them (je les aime) because they are kind and generous most of the time (la plupart du temps).

_____

_____

_____

3. Les réseaux sociaux
[Social media]

Word or phrase	Pronunciation guide	Aide-mémoire	English meaning	Tick
Compte (m)	kawnt	Just stick on an 'a'	Account	
Ajouter comme un ami	ah-zhouh-tay kawm ahn ah-mee	An **ad**junct is an add-on. Comme – like (**comm**on to all, like all, **as** all). Ami, as in amiable, amicable, friend.	Add as a friend	
Blog (m)	blog		Blog	
Fermer une session	fair-may oohn sess-yaw	Fermer, the verb to shut. F**e**rmly shut. 'Fermez la bouche', 'shut your mouth'. Shut a session.	Close a session	
Commentaire (m)	kaw-mawn-tair	Commentaire – commentary, comment	Comment	
Communauté (f)	kaw-moo-noh-tay	Communauté sounds like community	Community	
Contact (m)	kawn-takt		Contact	
Discussion (f)	deese-koo-see-yaw		Discussion	
Forum (m)	foh-rum		Forum	
S'identifier	see dawn-tee-fee-ay	Identify one**self**, log in	Log in	
Se déconnecter	seuh day-kawn-ek-tay	'Dé' can be used to mean 'dis' at the start of a word. Disconnect one**self**, log off.	Log off	
Se connecter	seuh kawn-ek-tay	Connect one**self**, log on	Log on	
Mot de passe (m)	moh deuh pass	Word of pass, mot, spoken by your **mo**uth	Password	
Profil (m)	proh-feel		Profile	
Photo (f) de profil	foh-toh deuh proh-feel		Profile picture	
Partager	pahr-tah-zhay	Divide into parts, **part**ager, share	Share	
Réseau(x) (m) social(aux)	ray-zoh soh-see-al	**R**o**ut**es connecting within society	Social network Social media	
Utilisateur, -trice (m/f)	ooh-tee-lee-zah-teuhr/treese	Utiliser, user	Username	

Practise!

Translate the following:

1. J'ai ajouté Bert comme un ami.

_____

_____

2. Ma photo de profil est terrible.

_____

_____

3. Je me suis connecté pour contacter mon ami.

_____

_____

4. Je n'ai pas pu me connecter car j'ai oublié le mot de passe.

_____

_____

5. J'ai partagé les informations en ligne.

_____

_____

6. I added Shane as a friend.

_____

_____

7. My profile picture is beautiful (belle).

_____

_____

4. Les nouvelles technologies
[New technologies]

Word or phrase	Pronunciation guide	Aide-mémoire	English meaning	Tick
Adresse (f)	ah-dress		Address	
Appli (f)	ah-plee	App is short for application. Appli is also short for application.	App	
Arobase (f)	ah-roh-bazz	The 'a' at the start helps and you will know it from context in an email address	At (the @ sign)	
Facture (f)	fak-toohr	Bills are **facts** of life	Bill	
Graver	grah-vay	To en**grave** information onto a disk is to burn it onto a disk	Burn	
Appeler	ah-pell-ay	To **appe**al to someone is to call out to them	Call	
Appareil-photo (m)	ah-pah-ray foh-toh	Apparatus for photo	Camera	
Cliquer	klee-kay	**Cli**quer	Click	
Disque (m) compact	deesk kom-pact		Compact disc	
Ordinateur (m)	oar-dee-nah-teuhr	Co-**ordinates** make computers work	Computer	
Ordi (m)	oar-dee	Short form of **ordi**nateur	Computer (slang)	
Brancher	braw-shay	A **branch** is connected to a limb, which is connected to the trunk of the tree	Connect, plug in	
Copier	caw-pee-ay		Copy	
Bureau (m)	booh-roh	Bureau, name for 'money changing office / bureau de change', desk in office	Desktop	
Télécharger	tay-lay-shaar-zhay	'Tele' means 'from a distance'. Charger – linked to cargo, a load, load from afar.	Download	
Courriel (m)	kouh-ree-el	**Courrie**rs deliver mail, in this case e-mail	E-mail	
Mél (m)	male	Looks like mail	E-mail	
Equipé (e/s) de	ay-keep-ay deuh		Equipped with	
Fichier (m)	fee-shee-ay	**Fi**le is linked	File	
Dossier (m)	doss-ee-ay	Dossier, in politics, e.g. a dossier on education, collection of documents	Folder	
Gratuit(e/s)	grah-too-ee	You are free to pay or not to pay a **gratuit**y. I am **grat**eful that it's free.	Free	
Jeu (m)	zheuh	Linked to jouer, to play. Joy of the game. Joyful jugglers.	Game	
Matériel (m)	mah-tay-ree-el	Raw **materiel** is **hard** to **ware** (wear) down	Hardware (computer)	
Internet (m)	ahn-tair-nett		Internet	
Site (m) internet	seet ah-tair-net		Internet site	
Informatique(s)	ah-fohr-mat-eek	**Informati**on technology	IT	
Clavier (m)	klah-vee-ay	Clavichord is a 17th century piano-type instrument, with a keyboard	Keyboard	
Ordinateur (m) portable	oar-dee-nah-teuhr pore-tah-bleuh	Portable computer (remember co-**ordinates** make computers work)	Laptop	

Word or phrase	Pronunciation guide	Aide-mémoire	English meaning	Tick
Lien (m)	lee-eh	**Lin**k	Link	
Clef (or clé) (f) USB	klay ooh ess bay	A **clef** is a key in music	Memory stick	
Portable (m)	pore-tah-bleuh	Portable phone	Mobile phone	
Souris (f)	souh-ree	The sound of the word is like a squeak, also the letters 'ous' are there	Mouse	
En ligne	awe-lee-nyeuh	E**n li**g**ne**	Online	
Coller	coll-ay	A **coll**age in art is pieces stuck (pasted) to a surface. La colle is glue, paste.	Paste	
Podcast (m)	pod-kahst		Podcast	
Poster	poss-tay		Post	
Imprimer	ahm-pree-may	To make an impression on a piece of paper is to print	Print	
Imprimante (f)	ahm-pree-mawnt	**Pri**nt is linked. Originally 'to impress' meant to print, make a print or impression.	Printer	
Projecteur (m)	proh-zhekt-eurr		Projector	
Mettre en ligne	met-reuh awe-leen-yeuh	Metteur-en-scène is a cinema director or putter-on-stage. An e**mitter** puts out signals.	Put online	
Sonnerie (f)	sawn-air-ee	**So**und, **ri**ng	Ringtone	
Sauvegarder	sohv-gaahr-day	Sauver – save, saviour. Garder – guard, look after.	Save	
Parabole (f)	pah-rah-bol	A parabola describes the shape of a satellite dish	Satellite dish	
GPS (m)	zhay pay ess	Géo-localisation Par Satellite OR Global Positioning System	Satnav	
Écran (m)	ay-kraw	'É' replaces an 's' at the start of a word. Therefore, scran, like screen.	Screen	
Envoyer	awe-vwhy-yay	A special **envoy** to a country is a diplomat sent to fulfil a political mission	Send	
Éteindre	ay-tahn-dreuh	Linked to **extin**guish, to turn, switch off	Shut down	
Carte (f) SIM	kaart seem		SIM card	
Logiciel (m)	loh-zhee-see-el	Programs come from **logic**	Software program	
Tableur (m)	tah-bleuhr	Tables are at the heart of spreadsheets	Spreadsheet	
En veille	awe vay-yeuh	Veille linked to 'wake'. When someone dies, people stay awake or **stand by** the body.	Stand-by	
Allumer	ah-loom-ay	Allumer, linked to i**llumin**ate, to switch on	Switch on	
Tablette (f)	tah-blet		Tablet	
Texto (m)	tex-toe		Text message	
Taper	tah-pay		Type	
Toile (f)	twaahl	A **t**ap**e**stry is a knitted hanging material, like a web	Web (spider's too)	
Wifi (m)	wee-fee		Wifi	

Practise!

Fill in the missing words in French. The words you need are in brackets, but in English:

1. One day I wanted _____ (to switch on) my _____ (laptop) but it

    wasn't possible because I hadn't paid my electricity _____ (bill).

2. When I paid my _____ (bill), I was able _____ (to plug in) my

    _____ (computer) and _____ (to switch on).

3. I was so happy because I was able _____ (to download) a

    _____ (software package), especially since it was

    _____ (free).

4. I love the _____ (web) because it is so easy to access stuff

    _____ (online).

5. One day, maybe a little further in the future, we will be able _____ (to download)

    _____ (a printer), _____ (a projector) and

    a _____ (SIM card). The only problem is that I keep on forgetting my

    _____ (username) and my _____ (password).

6. I really need a _____ (memory stick) that helps me to remember!

5: Les loisirs
[free time and leisure]

Word or phrase	Pronunciation guide	Aide-mémoire	English meaning	Tick
Film (m) d'aventure	feelm dah-vawn-toohr		Adventure film	
Publicité (f)	poo-blee-see-tay	**Publicise** information	Advertisement	
Article (m)	aarh-teek-leuh		Article	
Groupe (m)	grouhp		Group/ band	
Grand écran (m)	ay-kraw	'É' replaces an 's' at the start of a word. Therefore, scran, grand (big) screen.	Big screen	
Jeu (m) de société	zheuh deuh soh-see-ay-tay	Game social, social game, board game, played with others	Board game	
Livre (m)	lee-vreuh	A book has pages or 'leaves' and here is the link to **livre**	Book	
Brocante (m)	broh-kawnt	**Broke cawnt** be sold, unless you turn up to one of these, where you may sell	Car boot sale	
Dessin (m) animé	dess-ahn ahn-ee-may	Animated design	Cartoon	
Echecs (mpl)	ay-shek	'E' replaces an 's' at the start of a word, so **schec** sounds like the winning move (check)	Chess	
Cinéma (m) (aller au)	see-nay-mah		Cinema	
Clarinette (f)	klah-ree-net		Clarinet	
Musique (f) classique	moo-zeek clah-seek		Classic music	
Escalade (f) (faire de l')	ess-kah-lad	Escalade, escalator, to go up. **Scale** a mountain.	Climbing	
Film (m) comique	feel-meuh kaw-meek		Comedy film	
Bande (f) dessinée (la BD)	bawnd day-see-nay	A band, or a line of images, drawn (designed)	Comic book	
Concert (m)	kaw-sair		Concert	
Mots (mpl) croisés (faire des)	moh krwah-zay	**Croisé**s looks like **cros**sed. Mots – words, words come from the **mo**uth.	Crosswords	
Danse (f) (faire de la)	dawhss		Dancing	
Film (m) policier	feelm poh-lee-see-ay	Police film	Detective film	
Bricolage (m) (faire du)	bree-koh-lah-zheuh	If you do this, you lay your own **bric** at all**age**, young or old	DIY	
Numérique	noo-may-reek	Digital is all to do with binary **num**bers, digital, it's **numeri**cal	Digital	
Documentaire (m)	doh-koo-mawn-tair		Documentary	
Batterie (f)	bah-tree	You **beat** a drum	Drums	
Lecteur (m) DVD	lek-teuhr	Lecteurer, reader of a DVD, a reader plays the DVD	DVD player	
Écouteurs (mpl)	ay-kouh-teuhr	Écouter is the verb 'to listen', these are listeners	Earphones	

Word or phrase	Pronunciation guide	Aide-mémoire	English meaning	Tick
Film (m)	feelm		Film	
Écran (m) plat	ay-kraw	'É' replaces an 's' at the start of a word, so scran is like screen, a **plat**eau is flat	Flat screen	
Flute (f)	floot		Flute	
Jeu (m) télévisé	jeuh tay-lay-vee-zay	Game – from 'jouer'. Televised.	Game show	
Genre (m)	zhaw-reuh		Genre	
Guitare (f) (jouer de la)	gee-taahr		Guitar	
Casque (m)	kass-keuh	Great idea to put hearing devices in the cask on your head	Headphones	
Casque (m)	kass-keuh	Having a cask on your head will protect it	Helmet	
Film (m) d'horreur	feelm doh-reuhr		Horror film	
Film (m) d'épouvante	feelm day-pouh-vawnt	An épouvantail is a **scare**crow. 'é' at the start denotes 's', **spou**ky, horrifying.	Horror film	
Instrument (m)	ah-stroo-maw		Instrument	
Clavier (m)	klah-vee-ay	Clavichord is a 17th century piano-type instrument, with a keyboard	Keyboard	
Bibliothèque (m)	bee-blee-oh-tek	You can find a book called the Bible in this technical building	Library	
Magazine (m)	my-gah-zeen		Magazine	
Revue (f)	reuh-voo	A review is a magazine	Magazine	
Comédie (f) musicale	koh-may-dee moo-zee-kahl	It is not funny but a comédie can be simply a play, this one is musical	Musical	
Actualités (fpl)	ak-too-aal-eat-ay	**Actual**ly happening now – I want to find out about it, the news	News	
Informations (fpl)	ah-fohr-mass-yaw	New **information**s is actually news	News	
Journal (m)	jouhr-nahl	Each **day** (**jour**, as in bon-jour, good/**day**) one writes to complete the **jou**rnal	Newspaper	
Roman (m)	roh-maw	The first novels were **roman**ces. A novelist is a **roman**cier.	Novel	
Peinture (f) (faire de la)	pahn-toohr	Peinture, linked to **p**a**int**ing	Painting	
Piano (m) (jouer du)	pee-ah-no		Piano	
Musique (f) pop (écouter de la)	moo-zeek pop		Pop music	
Émission (f) sportive	ay-meese-yaw spor-teeve	Programmes are signals that are **emi**tted and these **emissions** are broadcasts	Programme (sport)	
Radio (f)	rah-dee-oh		Radio	
Rap (m)	rap		Rap	
Lecture (f)	lek-toohr	**Lecture**rs read from notes	Reading	
Musique (f) rock	moo-zeek rock		Rock music	
Série (f)	say-ree	**Seri**ously, you must see the link	Series	
Grasse matinée (f) faire la	grass mat-ee-nay (fair lah)	**Matinée**, early session in cinema, morning. **Grasse**, greasy, fat. 'Do the fat morning'.	Sleep in	

Word or phrase	Pronunciation guide	Aide-mémoire	English meaning	Tick		
Soirée pyjama	swah-ray pee-zhama	A soirée is a social evening party and pyjamas suggest the sleep element	Sleepover			
Chanteur (m), chanteuse (f)	shawn-teuhr, shawn-teuhz	**Chant**ing is singing	Singer			
Petit écran (m)	peuh-teet ay-kraw	**Petite** is used to describe a small girl, **petty** cash is small cash, 'é' replaces 's', so **scran**.	Small screen			
Feuilleton (m)	fay-yeuh-taw	Feuilles – pages, like in a port**folio**. These pages tell a soap opera, a story.	Soap opera			
Chanson (f)	shaw-saw	A **chan**t is a song	Song			
Film (m) sous-titré	feelm souh-teet-ray	**S**o**u**s – under, linked to sub, as in sub-marine, under water, under-titled	Subtitled film			
Chaine (f) de télé	shen deuh tay-lay	**Chan**nel is like **cha**ine	Television channel			
Trompette (f) (jouer de la)	trawm-pet	**Tr**om**pet**te	Trumpet (to play the)			
Voix (f)	vwah	**Voi**x looks like **voi**ce	Voice, a vote			
Météo (f)	may-tay-oh	**Météo** looks like **meteo**rological, which is to do with weather	Weather forecast			
Club (m) de jeunesse	kleuhb deuh zheuh-ness	Jeunesse is linked to **ju**v**en**ile, **jun**ior, youth	Youth club			

Practise!

Write, in French, what each sentence is referring to.

1. These are watched by those who follow stories on the television.

_____

2. These are projected with the voice in a melodic manner.

_____

3. This is a silent activity engaged in by a single person.

_____

4. This is a place where you don't find many seniors.

_____

5. Without this, musicians would find it difficult to use a piano.

_____

6. These are emitted in radio waves, and picked up by televisions.

_____

7. This is read on a daily basis in order to glean information.

_____

8. These are read by those who wish to follow a story, quietly.

_____

9. When you can't watch it on the big screen, it can be seen on this.

_____

10. Before I get on my motorbike, I will put this on.

_____

6: Les passetemps
(hobbies)

Word or phrase	Pronunciation guide	Aide-mémoire	English meaning	Tick
Passetemps (m)	pass-taw	Pass-time	Hobby	
Tchacher avec les amis	cha-chay ah-vek lays amee	Tchacher – chat. Amis – amicable, friendly.	Chat (online)	
Collectionner des timbres	collec-see-yawn-ay day tam-breuh	Collectionner – collect. Timbres – s**Tim**othy the s**Tam**p collector.	Collect stamps	
Faire du vélo	fair doo vay lo	Vélodrome is a cycling arena	Cycling	
Faire du shopping	fair doo shop-ping		Do shopping	
Dessiner	day-seen-ay	Design	Draw	
Faire des promenades	fair day prom-en-add	A promenade is a walkway by a beach	Go for a walk	
Aller en ville	aal-ay awe veal	Alley, you **go** down an alley. Ville – village?, no, a town.	Go into town	
Sortir avec mes amis	sore-teer ah-vek may zamee	Sort it **out** with your amiable friends	Go out with friends	
Faire des randonnées	fair day rawn-dawn-ay	**Ra**mbl**es** are walks	Go rambling	
Faire de la voile	fair deuh lah vwaal	A veil, like voile, is a piece of cloth, a big piece of cloth is a sail	Go sailing	
Faire de la plongée sous-marine	fair deuh lah plaw-zhay souh-maar-een	Plunging. Sous-marine – sub (under) marine (to do with the mer, sea).	Go scuba diving	
Aller au ciné	aal-ay oh see-nay		Go to the cinema	
Faire du cheval	fair doo sheuh-val	Cheval, chivalry, knights in shining armour. Knights ride horses.	Horse-riding	
Faire de l'équitation	fair deuh lay-key-tass-yaw	Equestrian, equine, to do with 'orses	Horse-riding	
Faire du footing	fair doo footing	Footing – jogging	Jogging	
Se maintenir en forme	seuh man-ten-ear awe form	Maintain form	Keep fit	
Écouter la musique	ay-kouh-tay lah moo-zeek	An echo is a sound that you listen for	Listen to music	
Faire du bruit	fair doo brwee	Brwee bang, boisterous, boing	Make noise	
Jouer au cricket	jouh-ay oh kreek-ett		Play cricket	
Jouer au golf	jouh-ay oh golf		Play golf	
Jouer de la guitare	jouh-ay deuh lah geet-aar		Play the guitar	
Jouer au hockey	jouh-ay oh awe-kay		Play hockey	
Jouer au rugby	jouh-ay oh roog-bee		Play rugby	
Jouer du piano	jouh-ay doo pee-ah-noh		Play the piano	
Faire des jeux (mpl) vidéo	fair day zheuh	Jouer – to play	Play video games	
Lire	lear	A **l**ectu**re** is a reading	Read	

Word or phrase	Pronunciation guide	Aide-mémoire	English meaning	Tick		
Vendre des choses	vawn-dreuh day shows	Vending machine, vendor. We chose our **things.** Mafia's motto 'Cosa nostra' means 'Our thing'.	Sell things			
Chanter	shawn-tay	Chanting is singing	Sing			
Rester dans la maison	res-tay daw la may-zaw	Staying at home for a rest. Maison – mansion – house – home.	Stay at home			
Faire de la natation	fair deuh la nat-tass-yaw	**Na**vy, **na**utical – to do with water	Swimming			
Nager dans la piscine	nah-zhay daw lah pea-seen	**Na**vy, **na**utical – to do with water. Piscine – this can happen in one!	Swim in the pool			
Nager dans la mer	nah-zhay daw lah mare	**Na**vy, **na**utical – to do with water. Mermaid – maid of the sea.	Swim in the sea			
Faire des photos	fair day foh-toh		Take photos			
Bronzer à côté de la piscine	ah coh-tay deuh la pea-seen	Côté – the 'ô' indicates an 's' after the o, so 'coste', like coast, like sea-**side**	Tan beside the pool			
S'entraîner au gymnase	sawn tren-ay oh zheem-nazz	S'en**train**er in the **gym**	Train in the gym			
Voyager	vwhy-aa-zhay	Voyage, travel	Travel			
Marcher dans les montagnes	maar-shay daw lay mawn-tah-nyeuh	Marching is walking	Walk in the mountains			
Regarder les films (mpl)	regard-ay lay feelm	With regard to something means 'looking at something', regarding you – looking at	Watch films			
Travailler dans le jardin	trav-eye-yeah daw leuh jaar-dah	To test ability to work, you are put on trial. 'travails' means 'work' in English, g(j)arde(i)n.	Work in the garden			

Practise!

Look at the translations below and add them in under the appropriate question and answer on the next page.

A. Quel est ton passe-temps favori? Moi, j'aime jouer aux jeux vidéo parce que je peux me reposer en faisant ça.

B. Qu'est-ce que tu aimes faire? J'aime jouer aux échecs car c'est un jeu dans lequel je dois penser.

C. Qu'est-ce que tu aimes faire? J'aime travailler dans le jardin car je le trouve reposant.

D. Qu'est-ce que tu aimes faire? J'aime voyager car je le trouve passionnant et je veux être journaliste.

E. Qu'est-ce que tu n'aimes pas faire? Je n'aime pas aller en ville car je le trouve coûteux et je n'aime pas perdre mon argent.

F. Qu'est-ce que tu n'aimes pas faire? Je n'aime pas travailler et je ne l'aime pas car je suis paresseux (paresseuse).

G. Qu'est-ce que tu n'aimes pas faire? Je n'aime pas dessiner étant donné que je suis nul en dessin.

H. Qu'est-ce que tu n'aimes pas faire? Je n'aime pas faire de l'équitation parce que je ne sais pas faire tourner le cheval.

1. What do you not like doing? I don't like going downtown because I find it expensive and I don't like losing my money.

   _____

   _____

2. What do you not like doing? I don't like drawing given that I am rubbish at art.

   _____

   _____

3. What do you like doing? I like travelling because I find it really interesting and I want to be a journalist.

   _____

   _____

4. What do you like doing? I like working in the garden because I find it relaxing.

   _____

   _____

5. What do you not like doing? I don't like horse-riding because I don't know how to make the horse turn.

   _____

   _____

6. What do you like doing? I like playing chess because it is a game in which I have to think.

   _____

   _____

7. What do you not like doing? I don't like working and I don't like it because I am lazy.

   _____

   _____

8. Which is your favourite hobby? Me, I like playing video games because I can relax by doing that.

   _____

   _____

7: Les animaux
[animals]

Word or phrase	Pronunciation guide	Aide-mémoire	English meaning	Tick
Animal (m)	ah-nee-maal		Animal	
Les animaux	lays ah-nee-moh		Animals	
Fourmi (f)	for-me	Ants walk **fourmi**les and **fourmi**les	Ant	
Abeille (f)	ah-bay-yeuh	Like our word, it has the same letters, **bee**, a**beille**	Bee	
Scarabée (m)	skah-rah-bay	The **scabb**y **scarab** beetle	Beetle	
Oiseau (m)	wah-zoh	**O**cean – bird flying over it. Flying over the **eau**, water. **Oi** (Wah!) **Seau** (So) (impressive).	Bird	
Perruche (f)	pair-oosh	Budgies love sitting on their **per**ru**ch**e	Budgie	
Bestiole (f)	best-ee-all	A wee **be**a**sti**e, bug	Bug	
Taureau (m)	tore-oh	The zodiac bull is **taur**us	Bull	
Papillon, (m)	pah-pee-yaw	The 'p's are wings, 'l's are antennae. It has a double consonant in middle like bu**tt**erfly.	Butterfly	
Chat (m)	shah	Remove the 'h'	Cat	
Vache (f)	vash	Term, '**vac**cine' because Jenner discovered milkmaids immune from cowpox	Cow	
Chien (m)	shee-yah	Canine	Dog	
Âne (m)	ahn	**A**ss. My donkey is called Âne.	Donkey	
Canard (m)	can-aar	Ducks doin' the can-can. Also 'can' is really the sound they make, not quack.	Duck	
Poisson (m)	pwah-saw	Pisces, poseidon	Fish	
Mouche (f)	mouhsh	They can end up as 'moush'	Fly	
Renard (f)	ren-aarh	**Ren**oune**d** for their deviousness	Fox	
Grenouille (f)	greuh-nouh-ee-yeuh	Frogs are **gre**en, **oui** (yes) they are. The **Fr**ench eat grenouille.	Frog	
Chèvre (f)	shev-reuh	Chevvie got chased by a goat. Chev your beard off, kid! Chevre my timbers, it's Billy!	Goat	
Poisson rouge	pwah-saw rouh-zheuh	English speakers see these fish as gold but the French are correct, they are red – rouge.	Goldfish	
Cochon d'Inde (m)	kaw-shaw daand	Something from India, (the English think they are from Guinea)	Guinea pig	
Hamster (m)	am-stair		Hamster	
Poule (f)	pouhl	Poultry	Hen	
Cheval (m)	sheuh-vaal	Chivalry is mannerly behaviour associated with knights – they ride horses	Horse	
Insecte (m)	ah-sekt		Insect	
Lézard (m)	lay-zaarh	**L**é**zard**	Lizard	
Singe, (m)	sah-zheuh	**Singe**d his hair **sw**i**ng**ing too close to the sun	Monkey	
Souris (f)	sou-ree	Squeaky rhymes	Mouse	
Perroquet (m)	pair-oh-kay	**Perro**quet looks like parrot, ok!	Parrot	
Cochon (m)	kaw-shaw	That thing from India or Guinea, check guinea pig	Pig	

Word or phrase	Pronunciation guide	Aide-mémoire	English meaning	Tick		
Lapin (m)	la-pah	If they could, they'd be 'lappin' up lettuce. Careful – it's pronounced 'la-pah'.	Rabbit			
Rat (m)	rah		Rat			
Mouton (m)	mou-taw	Mutton	Sheep			
Escargot (m)	ess-caar-go	Look how slow does the S Car Go!	Snail			
Serpent (m)	sair-paw	Another name for one	Snake			
Araignée (f)	aren-yay	Arachnophobia	Spider			
Crapaud (m)	krah-poh	There are some similar letters, crap**au**d. Both ugly sounding words. Toad in the hole.	Toad			
Tortue (f)	tore-too	More or less the same	Tortoise			
Guêpe (f)	gep	'Gep' off me!	Wasp			
Loup garou (m)	louh-garouh	Lupine means wolf-like, but it's not an ordinary wolf, **gar**d y**ou**rself!	Werewolf			
Loup (m)	louh	Lupine means wolf-like	Wolf			
Cloporte m	cloh-port	At night, they come through the door (la porte), (a sea port is a door to the land)	Woodlouse			

Practise!

1. Choose the fastest ten land animals and list them in French from the fastest to the slowest.
    (Choissisez les dix animaux de terre les plus vites et listez-les en français du plus vite au plus lent.)

    1. _____

    2. _____

    3. _____

    4. _____

    5. _____

    6. _____

    7. _____

    8. _____

    9. _____

    10. _____

2. Choose the fastest five flyers and list them in French from the fastest to the slowest.
(Choissisez les cinq volatiles les plus vites et listez-les en français du plus vite au plus lent.)

1. _____

2. _____

3. _____

4. _____

5. _____

3. Which are the animals here who like water?
(Quels sont les animaux ici qui aiment bien l'eau?)

1. _____

2. _____

3. _____

4. _____

8. Les achats et les vêtements
[Shopping and clothes]

Word or phrase	Pronunciation guide	Aide-mémoire	English meaning	Tick
Après-rasage (m)	ah-pray-rah-zah-zheuh	Après – after, as in après-ski – after skiing, **raz**or is linked to shaving	Aftershave	
Anorak (m)	ah-no-rak		Anorak	
Sac (m)	sak	Sack is a useful link	Bag	
Cagoule (f)	kah-gouhl	**Gh**o**uls** are scary and so are men in balaclavas	Balaclava	
Carte (f) bancaire	kaart bon-kair		Bank card	
Billet (m) de banque	bee-yay deuh bonk	Billet doux is a love note, if you remember that, you will remember this meaning	Banknote	
Ceinture (f)	saan-toohr	Goes around your **centre**	Belt	
Bottes (fpl)	bot		Boots	
Caleçon (m)	kah-less-awe	My **çon** called **Cale**b wears boxers	Boxers	
Soutien-gorge (m)	souh-tee-ah gor-zheuh	**S**o**us** (**su**b) – under. Tien – tenir, to hold (tenacious describes the ability to hold on, not give up). Gorge – valley, throat. 'Sous-tien gorge' – 'Hold the throat from below'.	Bra	
Casquette (f)	kas-kett	A little cask on your head won't protect you but it looks good, try it! Cask-it!	Cap	
Caisse (f)	kess	**Cas**h is dealt with here by the **cas**hier	Cash register	
Monnaie (f)	maw-nay	**Mone**y that jangles is change	Change	
Bon marché	baw maar-shay	Bon – good. Marché – market, for me, good market is cheap.	Cheap	
Vêtements (mpl)	vet-maw	The 'ê' means that the next letter is 's' so 'vest' is at the start of the word, clothing	Clothes	
Manteau (m)	maw-toh	A **man** wears it from his head to his **toe**, to keep off the water, **eau**	Coat	
Grand magasin (m)	graw mah-gah-zah	Grand – big. Magasin – linked to **ma**rket, **m**erchan**t**, shop, big shop, deptartment store.	Department store	
Robe (f)	rob	A robe is a dress, e.g. wedding robe	Dress	
Cher/s, chère/s	shair	You **cher**ish your loved ones, they are **dear**ly loved, dear is expensive	Expensive	
Pêche (f)	pesh	**Pis**c**e**s is the zodiac sign for the fish, **p**o**se**idon is the god of the sea	Fishing	
Gant (m)	gaw	To throw down the **ga**u**nt**let! means challenge! Literally, throw down the glove.	Gloves	
Or (m)	or	El D**or**ado is the name of a town during the gold rush. Also aur**or**a, golden.	Gold	
Sac (m) à mains	sak-ah-mah	**Sac**k is bag. **Man**ipulate is to **hand**le.	Handbag	
Chapeau (m)	shap-oh	A **chap** wears this to keep water (**eau**) off his head	Hat	
Sweat (m) à capuche	sweet ah kah-poosh	Sweat from sweatshirt, hoodie material. **Cap**uccino, hood of foam on the coffee.	Hoodie	
Blouson (m)	blouh-zaw	A jacket is like a blouse, worn on one's top half to protect from the cold	Jacket	

Word or phrase	Pronunciation guide	Aide-mémoire	English meaning	Tick		
Veste (f)	vest	A very thick vest is a jacket	Dress jacket			
Jean (m)	jean		Jeans			
Bijoux (mpl)	bee-zhouh	Bi**jou**-wellry	Jewellery			
Pull (m)	pool	**Pull**-over	Jumper			
Cuir (m)	kweer	Leather would be a **cuir** thing to wear to a wedding	Leather			
Maquillage (m)	mah-kee-ah-zheuh	**Maq**-up in order to hide your -**age**	Make-up			
Match (m)	match		Match			
Rendez-vous (m)	rawn-day-vouh	A rendez-vous can be found in an English dictionary to mean meeting	Meeting, date			
Argent (m)	aahr-zhaw	Argento, a shop that sells silver. Chemical symbol Ag. Pieces of silver are money.	Money, silver			
Culotte (f)	koo-lot	Girls wear culottes which are close to being pants, sort of…, at least they go on the bum.	Pants (for women)			
Slip (m)	sleep	Slip on your pants, men!	Pants (for men)			
Peinture (f)	pahn-toohr	**Peint**ure, looks like painting	Painting			
Parfum (m)	par-fah		Perfume			
Cadeau (m)	kaa-doh	The golfer gave a **cadeau** to thank his **cad**die	Present			
Porte-monnaie (m)	port-monn-ay	**Porte**rs carry things for customers. Here we have a **porte**r of **mon**nai**ey**.	Purse			
Reçu, ticket de caisse	reuh-soo, tee-kay deuh kess	A **rec**eipt, is **rec**eived, it is a **ticket** from the **cas**hier, from the till	Receipt			
Sandales (fpl)	sawn-dahl		Sandals			
Écharpe (f)	ay-sharp	'É' replaces an 's'at the start of a word, this gives us 'scharp'	Scarf			
Short (m)	short		Shorts			
Imperméable (f)	ahm-pair-may-able	If it's **imperméable**, water will not get through it	Raincoat			
Soldes (fpl)	salld	**Sold** in the sales	Sales			
Chemise (f)	sheuh-meeze	**Sh**emi**s**e, short of shounds like shirt	Shirt			
Chemisier	sheuh-mee-zee-ay	Chemisier, closely linked to shirt but strangely, without the ending in 'e', it is a shirt for girls	Shirt (blouse)			
Chaussures (fpl)	show-soorh	A **cause**way, a road you **walk** on, linked to **chauss**ures.	Shoes			
Magasin (m)	mah-gah-zah	**M**erch**an**ts work from shops, **ma**rkets are shops without ceilings	Shop			
Centre commercial (m)	sawn-treuh kaw-mair-see-al	Commercial centre	Shopping centre			
Spectacle (m)	spek-tak-leuh	A spectacle is a show, watched by spectators	Show			
Soie (f)	swah	A little link between the two four letter words, **si**lk, **soi**e. A **sua**ve fabric.	Silk			
Skate (m)	skate		Skateboarding			
Jupe (f)	zhoop	This is the sound of the zip on the side of the zhoop	Skirt			
Chaussettes (fpl)	show-set	Little things, 'ettes' little shoes, **chauss**ettes, link to **cause**way, feet, walking	Socks			
Souvenir (m)	souh-ven-eer		Souvenir			

Word or phrase	Pronunciation guide	Aide-mémoire	English meaning	Tick
Maillot (m) de bain	my-yoh-deuh-bah	A coat of **mail**, worn in the Middle Ages to protect. This is a **ba**thing coat of **mail**.	Swim costume	
T-shirt (m)	tee-shirt		T-shirt	
Théâtre (m)	tay-ah-treuh		Theatre	
Parc (m) d'attractions	park dah-trak-see-yaw	Various **attractions** at a theme park	Theme park	
Cravate (f)	krah-vat	A cravate is a sort of scarf/tie in English	Tie	
Articles (mpl) de toilette	aarh-teek-leuh deuh twah-let	Here toilet means everything you do in the bathroom except go to the toilet	Toiletries	
Produits (mpl) de toilette	proh-dwee deuh twah-let	**Produ**cts for everything you do in the bathroom except go to the toilet	Toiletries	
Jouet (m)	jouh-way	The **jo**y that comes from a toy	Toy	
Baskets (fpl)	basket	These shoes are used to play **basket**ball	Trainers	
Pantalon (m)	pawn-tah-law	**Pantalo**ons are a type of trousers	Trousers	
Maillot (m)	my-yoh	A coat of **mail**, worn in the Middle Ages to protect. This **mail**lot protects from the cold.	Undershirt	
Portefeuille (m)	pore-teuh-fay-yeuh	Porters carry things, here it is feuilles, leaves. A **port folio** a big art wallet.	Wallet	
Montre (f)	mawn-treuh	This device de**mon**st**ra**tes the time. A **mont**age shows things, here the time.	Watch	
Laine (f)	len	Bah Bah mouton noir, as-tu de la laine? Oui Monsieur, Oui Monsieur, trois sacoches pleines.	Wool	
Bonnet (m)	baw-nay	A bonnet is a hat. In French it is woolly.	Woolly hat	

Practise!

1. Make a list of the ten things that could be the most expensive, from the most to least expensive.
   (Faites une liste des dix choses qui pourraient être les plus chères, de la plus chère à la moins chère.)

   1. _____

   2. _____

   3. _____

   4. _____

   5. _____

   6. _____

   7. _____

   8. _____

   9. _____

   10. _____

2. Make an **alphabetic** (using the French) list of clothing from left to right, using at least ten words and attaching one piece of clothing to the next without leaving a space between them. When you have finished, see if you can read the combination out loud! It has been started for you:

Basketsbottes

9. La bijouterie
(The Jewellery shop)   **(Not on the CCEA core vocabulary list)**

Word or phrase	Pronunciation guide	Aide-mémoire	English meaning	Tick
Piercing du nombril (m)	peer-sing doo nawm-breel	**N**ave**l** is linked to **n**ombri**l**, n**om**bril is in the st**om**ach, or the **bel**ly	Belly piercing	
Bracelet (m)	brass-lay		Bracelet	
Boucle d'oreille (f)	bouh-kleuh doh-ray-yeuh	**Aur**al, oreille, to do with listening. **Buckle**, a buckle in the ear.	Earring	
L'eau de toilette (f)	loh deuh twah-let	Eau, aqua, water. Toilette in this expression is not to do with a lavatory. Here, one's toilette is one's ablutions, grooming. So this is grooming water, perfume (eau de Cologne).	Eau de toilette	
Bague (f) de fiançailles	bahg deuh fee-awn-sye	Get a husband and **bague** yourself a ring. The name of the one to whom you are engaged is your fiancé (m) or your fiancée (f).	Engagement ring	
Paupières (fpl)	poh-pee-air	Jeepers, creepers, where d'ya get those **pee**pe**rs**, where d'ya get those eyes?	Eyelids	
Fausses ongles (m)	fohsse awn-gleuh	Fausse, **fa**l**se** a**ngu**lar extensions to fingers	Fake nails	
Faux cils (mpl)	foh seel	Faux – **fa**lse. False eyelashes seal (cil) the deal!	False eyelashes	
Fard (m)	Faahr	**F**o**un**d**a**tion	Foundation	
Or (m)	Orr	Gold **or**e, material from which gold produced. El D**or**ado, town where gold was found.	Gold	
Bijouterie (f)	bee-jouh-tree	The 'jew' sound is there, bi**jou**, also the shop ending, -**erie**, like bak**ery**	Jewellers	
Rouge à lèvres (m)	rouh-zheuh ah lev-reuh	Rouge is the name for red cheek make-up in English. Red for l**èvre**s, l**ips**.	Lipstick	
Maquillage (m)	mah-kee-ah-zheuh	**Ma**q**uillage** – **ma**k**e**-up. Le **Maqui**s, Resistance during Second World War, who used camouflage.	Make-up	
Vernis à ongles (m)	vair-nee ah awn-gleuh	**Ve**r**nis** varnish or polish for the **ang**u**l**ar bits at the end of the fingers	Nail polish	
Collier (m)	kawl-yay	**Coll**ar round the neck	Necklace	
Piercing du nez (m)	peer-sing doo nay	Nez, nasal, nose	Nose piercing	
Parfum (m)	paahr-fah	Parfum means perfume or flavour (crisps etc)	Perfume	
Bague (f)	Bahg	Get a husband and **bague** yourself a ring	Ring (for finger)	
Anneau (m)	ah-noh	The **anu**s is a ring	Ring (generic)	
Argent (m)	aahr-zhaw	Chemical symbol, **Ag** for silver, 'Argento' is the name of a jeweller's	Silver, money	
Lunettes (fpl) de soleil	loo-net deuh soh-lay	Little moon-shaped lenses, lunettes, solaire, to do with the sun	Sunglasses	
Alliance (f)	ah-lee-awnse	An alliance is a partnership, symbolised by this ring	Wedding ring	

Practise!

1. Make an **alphabetic** (using the French) list of items from the above list from left to right, using at least six words and attaching one word to the next without leaving a space between them. When you have finished, see if you can read the combination out loud!

10: La papetrie
[the stationery shop]   [Not on the CCEA core vocabulary list]

Word or phrase	Pronunciation guide	Aide-mémoire	English meaning	Tick
Calculette (f)	kahl-kooh-let		Calculator	
Journal (m) intime	jouhr-naahl ahn-teem	Bonjour! Goodday! Journal, daily, intimate details for sharing with no-one.	Diary (Dear Diary)	
Cahier (m)	kye-yay	Cahier – linked to **ca**lendar, where you write things down	Exercise book	
Perce-trou (m)	pairse-trouh	Percer is the verb to pierce. Trou – h**o**le, a word which has an 'o', like a h**o**le.	Hole punch	
Carnet (m) de devoirs	ka ahr-nay deuh deuhv-waahr	**Car**net linked to **ca**lendar where we write things like our '**dev**oirs' – **dut**ies, homework.	Homework diary	
Feutre (m)	feuh-treuh	**Feu**tre – link with **fe**lt tip pen, marker pen	Marker pen	
Papier (m)	pah-pee-yay		Paper	
Stylo (m)	stee-loh	A stylus is the bit at the end of a pen with which one writes	Pen	
Crayon (m)	kray-yaw	Crayon and pencil, big link	Pencil	
Photocopieuse (f)	foh-toh-kop-ee-yeuhze	-euse describes the machine. The word machine is feminine. **Une** machine photocopi**euse**.	Photocopier	
Projecteur (m)	proh-zhek-teuhr		Projector	
Règle (f)	reh-gleuh	A ruler, a king or queen, is **reg**al	Ruler	
Agrafeuse (f)	ah-grah-feuhze	-euse, feminine ending, describes la machine a**gra**feuse. Staple **gra**pples two pages together.	Stapler	
Papetrie (f)	pah-pet-ree	Paper shop, remember, -rie denotes a shop, e.g. boulange**rie** (bak**ery**)	Stationers	
Livre (m) de texte	lee-vreuh deuh text	Livre – link to lever arch file or leaflet	Textbook	
Carnet (m) de vocabulaire	kaahr-nay deuh voh-kah-booh-lair	**Car**net is linked to **ca**lendar in which we write things	Vocabulary notebook	
Tableau (m) blanc	tah-bloh blaw	Tableau – link to tablet, which is a board. Blanc – white, link to blank, white.	Whiteboard	

Practise!

1. List (in French) what you think are the five most environmentally unfriendly articles in this list, saying why you think this (in English).

_____ Raison: _____

_____ Raison: _____

_____ Raison: _____

_____ Raison: _____

_____ Raison: _____

11: La routine quotidienne
(Daily routine)

Word or phrase	Pronunciation guide	Aide-mémoire	English meaning	Tick		
Goûter (m)	gouh-tay	Dis**gust** means to not enjoy tasting, **g**oûter is to enjoy tasting. Taste, then off to the **gût**.	Afternoon snack			
Réveil (m)	ray-vay	**Revi**val, wakes you up	Alarm clock			
À la maison	ah lah may-zaw	In the **man**sion	At home			
Chez moi	shay mwah	Come and shtay shay mwah! Shay, you wanna shtay shay mwah?	At my house			
Petit déjeuner (m)	peuh-tee day-zheuh-nay	Petit – small (petty cash). Jeuner – to fast, dé in front verb reverses it, break-fast.	Breakfast			
Pause-café (f)	poze-kah-fay	Pause for coffee	Coffee break			
Routine (f) quotidienne	rouh-teen koh-tee-dee-yenn	Quoti**di**en, from lun**di**, mar**di** etc. Quotidian allowance – daily payment.	Daily routine			
Dîner (m)	dee-nay		Dinner, evening meal			
Tôt	Toe	À bien**tôt** – until well **early**. Which gets up first, **to**e or **ear**? The 'ô' denotes 's' after 'o', **toa**st, early morning food.	Early			
Brosse à cheveux (f)	bross-ah-sheuh-veuh	**Bros**se looks like brush. Cheveux is hair, we know that!	Hairbrush			
L'après-midi	lah pray-mee-dee	Après-ski is after skiing. Midi is midday, lun-di, mar-di, mi-di, after-noon.	In the afternoon			
Le soir	leuh swahr	Soir is like soirée, an evening gathering, so soir is evening	In the evening			
Le matin	leuh mah-tah	Sonnez les matines – the bells rung in the morning, matinée is an early cinema showing.	In the morning			
Tard	Taarh	If something is tardy, it is late	Late			
En retard	awe reuh-taarh	Retarded is delayed in terms of development	Late (delayed)			
Maintenant	mah-teuh-naw	Main (manipulate, hand), tenant (holding). With hand held out, money **now** please!	Now			
Quotidiennement	koh-tee-dee-yeah, koh-tee-dee-yenn	Quoti**di**en, from lun**di**, mar**di** etc. Quotidian allowance – daily payment.	On a daily basis			
Le lundi	leuh lahn-dee	Lun – lunar, Mon – moon. Moonday is Lunday. Rememmember that **Le** lundi, **the** Monday means **on** Monday.	On Monday(s)			
Souvent	souh-vaw	The letters, **o t e n** are hidden in this word – and so **often** they aren't seen!	Often			
Aujourd'hui	oh-jouhr-dwee	Literally (au) **at the** (jour) **day** (de) **of** (hui) 'hodie', Latin for **today**.	Today			
Demain	deuh-mah	De**main** – linked to Spanish for tomorrow, mañana. Mañana mañana! Do it tomorrow.	Tomorrow			
Brosse à dents (f)	bross-ah-daw	A brush for dentures	Toothbrush			
Hier	ee-yair	The 'yeuh' sound is in the pronunciation for the word, as is the 'er' sound, **yeuh** st**er** day	Yesterday			

Practise!

1. Join each phrase on the left to the appropriate phrase on the right to make sense. The first one has been done for you.

1. Je me brosse les dents

2. Le lundi

3. Demain est

4. L'homme qui n'a pas de cheveux

5. Quand je rentre de l'école

6. Je me lève le matin

A. le jour après aujourd'hui

B. je dois me lever tôt pour l'école

C. quotidiennement

D. je prends mon goûter car j'ai faim

E. n'utilise pas la brosse à cheveux

F. et je me couche le soir

2. Translate each of the completed sentences from question 1 into English below. The first one has been done for you.

1. I brush my teeth on a daily basis _____

2. _____

3. _____

4. _____

5. _____

6. _____

12: La routine quotidienne – quelques verbes
[Daily Routine – some verbs]

Word or phrase	Pronunciation guide	Aide-mémoire	English meaning	Tick
Arriver à l'école	ah-ree-vay ah lay-koll	The 'é' at the start of a word replaces an 's' – scol – scholar, school	Arrive in school	
Avoir froid	ah-vwaahr fr-wah	Birds (h)**av**(e)-**wire** under their claws. **Frid**ge, cold.	Be cold (have cold)	
Avoir chaud	ah-vwaahr show	Birds (h)**av**(e)-**wire** under their claws. **Chau**ffeur warms the car for lady.	Be hot (have hot)	
Avoir faim	ah-vwaahr fah	Birds (h)**av**(e)-**wire** under their claws. **Fam**ine, **fam**ished.	Be hungry (have hunger)	
Avoir soif	ah-vwaahr swaff	Birds (h)**av**(e)-**wire** under their claws. To quaff a drink means to gulp. Qwaff, swaff.	Be thirsty (have thirst)	
Brosser les dents (se)	brass-ay lay daw	**Bross**er, like brush, dent, dentist, teeth	Brush one's teeth	
Habiller (s')	ah-bee-yay	A monk's habit is his gown. Get into a habit, get into your clothes, dress.	Dress	
Boire	Bwaahr	A **b**ev**er**age is a drink	Drink	
Manger le petit-déjeuner	maw-zhay leuh peuh-tee day-zheuh-nay	Cattle eat from a manger. Petit (small), déjeuner (jeûner 'to fast', dé breaks it).	Eat breakfast	
Manger	maw-zhay	Cattle eat from a manger	Eat	
Terminer les cours	tair-mee-nay lay couhr	Terminate means to bring to an end. The terminus is the end destination of a bus.	End / finish classes	
Préparer (se)	pray-pah-ray	Prepared, ready	Get ready	
Lever	leuh-vay	E**lev**ate, lever up something	Get up	
Aller au lit	ah-lay oh lee	The candle is 'lit' and I am going to bed	Go to bed	
Coucher (se)	kouh-shay	Lie down on the **couch**	Go to bed (lie down)	
Descendre (en bas)	des-sawn-dreuh	Descending is going down (**bas**s – low, down)	Go downstairs	
Faire une ballade	fair-oon-bah-lad	Whistle a ballad while going on a stroll	Go for a walk	
Rentrer à la maison	rawn-tray ah lah may-zaw	Re-enter home is to go back home. Maison – mansion – house – home.	Go home	
Aller en cours	ah-lay awe kouhr	A course at University is a class	Go to class	
Aller à l'école à pied	ah-lay ah lay-koll ah pee-yay	Go down an **alle**y. The 'é' replaces the 's', so **s**cole, school. À pied – on foot, **ped**estrian, foot.	Go to school on foot	
Monter (en haut)	mawn-tay	Up a **mo**u**nt**ain (haut – **h**igh, **hau**ghty, up)	Go upstairs	
Prendre le petit déjeuner	prawn-dr leuh peuh tee day-zheuhn-ay	Entre**prendre** – 'to under**take**', to undertake a project. From entreprendre, we have entrepreneur, une entreprise (an undertaking, business). Petit, petty, small. Jeûner, to fast, dé-jeuner, break fast.	Have (take) breakfast	
Quitter la maison	kee-tay lah may-zaw	Quit – stop or **leave** behind, maison – mansion – house	Leave the house	
Mettre des vêtements	mett-reuh day vet-maw	To e**mit** rays, to **put** out rays, to o**mit**, to fail to **put**. Vêt – 'ê' becomes 's', vest, clothing.	Put on clothes	

Word or phrase	Pronunciation guide	Aide-mémoire	English meaning	Tick
Maquiller (se)	mak-ee-yay	Mak-ee up – yay! During the Second World War, the Maquis, the Resistance, wore camouflage.	Put on make-up	
Raser (se)	rah-zay	Razor, shaver, shave	Shave	
Dormir	door-mear	Dormitory a place where you sleep, dormant, a sleeping volcano	Sleep	
Parler avec mes amis	par-lay ah-vek mays ah-mee	Parlour is a room where you speak, parlance is a way of speaking	Speak with friends	
Commencer les cours	cawm-awse-ay lay kouhr	Commence is the same as start	Start classes	
Prendre une douche	prawn-dr oon douh-sh	Entre**prendre** means 'to under**take**'. A douh-shh – sound of a bucket emptying.	Take a shower	
Prendre le bus	prawn-dreuh le bousse	A preneur is a **taker**, as in entrepreneur, someone who under**takes** to do something.	Take (get) the bus	
Déshabiller (se)	day=zah-bee-yay	A monk's habit is his gown. Get into a habit, dress. Dé – reversess, so un-dress.	Undress	
Attendre	ah-tawn-dreuh	If a lady in **wait**ing is **attend**ing to her mistress, she is doing her job	Wait	
Réveiller (se)	ray-vay-yay	Revive	Wake up	
Promener le chien	prom-en-ay leuh shee-yeah	A promenade is a walkway by the beach	Walk the dog	
Laver	lah-vay	**Lav**atory, **la**undry – to do with water	Wash	
Travailler en classe	trah-vye-yeah awe class	Travail is an old word for hardship, work	Work in class	

Practise!

Choose 16 of the actions given in the table above and list them in chronological order. Either use the present tense (Je me réveille à sept heures et demie) or simply use the infinitive (réveiller). Provide the English too.

Example

Je me réveille à sept heures et demie   OR   se réveiller _____

English: I wake up at 7.30 OR to wake up _____

1. _____

English : _____

2. _____

English : _____

3. _____

English : _____

4. _____

English : _____

5. _____

English : _____

6. _____

English : _____

7. _____

English : _____

8. _____

English : _____

9. _____

English : _____

10. _____

English : _____

11. _____

English : _____

12. _____

English : _____

13. _____

English : _____

14. _____

English : _____

15. _____

English : _____

16. _____

English : _____

13: Les coutumes, les fêtes et les célébrations
[Customs, festivals and celebrations]

Word or phrase	Pronunciation guide	Aide-mémoire	English meaning	Tick
Poisson d'avril (m)	pwah-saw dah-vreel	Poisson, **pis**ces from zodiac, **Pos**eid**on**, god of the sea. You look like a fool with fish on your back.	April Fools' Day	
Jour férié (m)	jouhr fay-ree-ay	Jour – day, as in daily **jour**nal. **Fé**rié – linked to **fe**stival. Banks take festival days off.	Bank holiday	
Baptême (m)	bah-tem	**Bapt**ême, looks like baptism. Also, the 'ê' tells us that an 's' comes after the 'ê'.	Baptism	
Fête (f) nationale	fet nah-see-yawn-al	Fête is used to mean garden party in English. Also, 'ê' tells us that an 's' comes after, so 'feast'.	National/ Bastille Day	
Naître	nett-reuh	Nativity, natal to do with birth	Be born	
Naissance (f)	nay-soss	Nativity, natal to do with birth	Birth	
Anniversaire (m)	ah-nee-vair-sair	Birthdays take place on the anniversary of one's birth	Birthday	
Enterrement (m)	awe-tair-maw	The 'terr', in the word, 'enterrement' is linked to territory, terrain, earth. **En terr** in earth, buried.	Burial	
Bougies (fpl)	bouh-zhee	Budgies are yellow, so is the flame of a candle! Repeat this phrase, it burns it into your head.	Candles	
Carte (f)	kaart	**Ca**rte sounds and looks like card	Card	
Fêter	fet-ay	'Ê' tells us that an 's' comes after, so 'feast'. To feast is to celebrate or party. (Garden party, fête).	Celebrate	
Église (f)	ay-gleese	**Ec**cl**es**iastical, which means 'to do with the church' is linked to église	church	
Noël (m)	noh-ell	Noël Noël Noël Noël, born is the King of Israël	Christmas	
Réveillon (m) de Noël	ray-vay-yaw	Réveillon signifies staying awake (**révei**l, **revi**ve), the night before. Also, note 'eve' is in r**éve**illon.	Christmas Eve	
La veille de Noël	lah-vay-yeuh de no-well	A funeral **wa**ke, a tradition, one stays awake with the body the eve of funeral. **V**ei**lle**, **wa**ke, **eve**.	Christmas Eve	
Mort (f)	mohr	Mortuary, morgue, post-mortem, all linked to death	Death	
Mort (m)	mohr	Mortuary, morgue, post-mortem, all linked to death	Dead person	
Décorer			Decorate	
Mourir	mouh-reer	Mortuary, morgue, post-mortem, all linked to death	Die	
Pâques (fpl)	pak	**Pâqu**es means **Pass**ov**er**. It is a Jewish Spring Festival. Easter is at Springtime.	Easter	
Fiançailles (f)	fee-awe-sye	When you are engaged, you are **fiancés**. Obvious link to **fianç**ail**les**.	Engagement	
Jeûner	zheuh-nay	Déjeuner, the opposite of jeûner. Dé reverses a verb, to **break**fast. Jeune, junior, youth, fast!	Fast	
Père (m) Noël	pair noh-well	Papa, paternal, linked to father. Noël means birth, here birth of Christ, as in 'the first Noël'.	Father Christmas	
Drapeau (m)	drah-poh	A drape is a sheet. A flag is a coloured sheet. **Drape, drapea**u.	Flag	
Feux (mpl) d'artifice	feuh daar-tee-feese	Artificial **fi**re (**fe**u). That is what fireworks are.	Fireworks	

Word or phrase	Pronunciation guide	Aide-mémoire	English meaning	Tick		
Bon anniversaire	bonn ah-nee-vair-sair	Good anniversary	Happy Birthday			
Toussaint (f)	lah touh-sah	Tous – total. Saint – saints. Hallowe'en is a celebration of All Saints' Day.	Hallowe'en			
Cadeau (m)	kah-doh	**Ca** comes from the **ca**rd that accompanies the gift. **Deau**, pronounces 'doh' linked to **do**nate, give.	Gift			
Donner	daw-nay	To **don**ate is to give	Give			
Offrir	off-reer	To **off**er is to give. Used with a present in French. 'Je t'offre un cadeau' – 'I give you a present'.	Give (offer) a gift			
Lumières (fpl)	loo-mee-yair	**Illumi**nat**es** and **Illumi**nation**s** are linked. In Beauty and the Beast there is a candle named Lumière.	Lights			
Messe (f)	mess	Close obvious link, messe and **m**a**ss**	Mass			
Défilé (m)	day-fee-lay	When a battalion, or a bank, **file**s past, they march past	March (as in a parade)			
Joyeux Noël	zhwy-yeux noh-well	**Joy**o**u**s means merry. Noël – Christmas.	Merry Christmas			
Mosquée (f)	moss-kay		Mosque			
Nouvel An (m)	nouh-vel awe	Nouvel is linked to 'novice', 'renewal', new. 'An' is linked to **an**nual, yearly.	New Year			
Saint Sylvestre (f)	sah seel-vest-reuh	Saint Sylvester was a Pope who died on the 31st December 358.	New Year's Eve			
Boum (f)	bouhm	This is the sound of the music at the party. It is a young adolescent's party. Boum boum boum.	Party			
Ramadan (m)	rah-mah-daw		Ramadan			
Recevoir	reuh-seuh-vwaahr		Receive			
Envoyer	awe-vwy-ay	A special **envoy** is a journalist **sent** to a foreign place to report	Send			
Mardi gras (m)	maar-dee grah	**Greasy** Tuesday, when pancakes are made, with **butter**, to use up flower and eggs before fasting	Shrove Tuesday			
Synagogue (f)	see-nah-gog		Synagogue			
Mariage (m)	mah-ree-ah-zheuh		Wedding			
Souhaiter	souh-wet-ay	I **wish** I wasn't so **souhaiter**. Said by perspiring person. À tes souhaits, to your wishes, bless you!	Wish			

Practise!

Which words are being described?

1. Deux mots différents pour signifier le jour avant Noël.

   _____ _____

2. Un verbe qui est utilisé pour signifier 'donner' pour les cadeaux.

   _____

3. Un verbe qui nous donne le nom (a verb which gives us the noun), « réception » .

   _____

4. Des vacances quand il y a les sorcières et les masques et les feux d'artifices.

   la T_____

5. C'est le prénom d'un garçon et le nom d'un festival de fin décembre.

   _____

6. C'est une période de temps avant le mariage.

   _____

7. C'est le jour où on mange les crêpes.

   _____

8. C'est le nom des vacances que nous avons au mois de mars ou avril.

   _____

9. En Irlande du Nord, le douze juillet, les orangistes font un grand:

   _____

10. Deux verbes qui sont les contraires, les opposés.

   M_____ opposé à N_____

11. Une période de l'année dans la religion musulmane quand on ne mange pas.

_____

12. Quand c'est ton anniversaire, normalement, tu reçois un:

_____

13. C'est un bâtiment important dans la religion musulmane.

M __ __ Q __ __ __

14. C'est un bâtiment important dans la religion juive.

SY __ __ __ __ G __ __